TOM BRADY

Pete DiPrimio

Mitchell Lane
PUBLISHERS

P.O. Box 196
Hockessin, Delaware 19707
Visit us on the web: www.mitchelllane.com
Comments? email us: mitchelllane@mitchelllane.com

Mitchell Lane PUBLISHERS

Printing   1   2   3   4   5   6   7   8   9

A Robbie Reader
Contemporary Biography

Albert Pujols	Alex Rodriguez	Aly and AJ
Amanda Bynes	Ashley Tisdale	Brittany Murphy
Charles Schulz	Dakota Fanning	Dale Earnhardt Jr.
Donovan McNabb	Drake Bell & Josh Peck	Dr. Seuss
Dwayne "The Rock" Johnson	Dylan & Cole Sprouse	Eli Manning
Hilary Duff	Jamie Lynn Spears	Jessie McCartney
Johnny Gruelle	Jonas Brothers	Jordin Sparks
LeBron James	Mia Hamm	Miley Cyrus
Miranda Cosgrove	Raven Symone	Shaquille O'Neal
The Story of Harley-Davidson	Syd Hoff	Tiki Barber
Tom Brady	Tony Hawk	

Library of Congress Cataloging-in-Publication Data
DiPrimio, Pete.
  Tom Brady / by Pete DiPrimio.
      p. cm. — (A Robbie reader)
  Includes bibliographical references and index.
  ISBN 978-1-58415-718-2 (library bound)
  1. Brady, Tom, 1977– 2. Football players—United States—Biography—Juvenile literature. 3. Quarterbacks (Football)—United States—Biography—Juvenile literature.
I. Title.
  GV939.B685D56 2009
  796.332092—dc22
  [B]
                                                                        2008008074

ABOUT THE AUTHOR: Pete DiPrimio is a veteran sports columnist for the *Fort Wayne [Indiana] News-Sentinel,* a long-time freelance feature, fiction, and travel writer. He is the author of three nonfiction books pertaining to Indiana University athletics and of *Eli Manning* by Mitchell Lane Publishers.

PHOTO CREDITS: Cover, pp. 4—Paul Spinelli/Getty Images; p. 7—Harry How/Getty Images; p. 8—Gabriel Bouys/AFP/Getty Images; p. 10—AP Photo/Scott Audette; p. 13—James D. Smith/WireImage.com; p. 14—Roberto Schmidt/AFP/Getty Images; p. 16—AP Photo/Winslow Townson; p. 17—John Mottern/AFP/Getty Images; p. 18—AP Photo/Pat Sullivan; p. 20—Arthur Anderson/WireImage.com; p. 22—AP Photo/Peter Cosgrove; p. 24—AP Photo/Ronen Zilberman; p. 27—John Barrett/Globe Photos.

TABLE OF CONTENTS

Words in **bold** type can be found in the glossary.

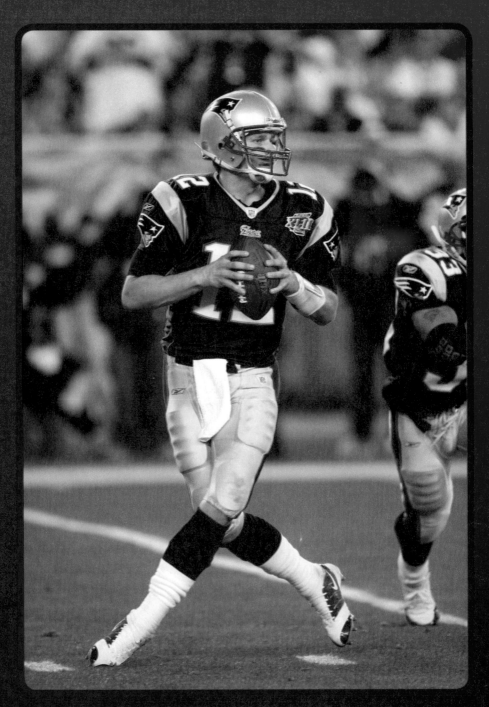
Tom Brady looks for an open receiver against the New York Giants in Super Bowl XLII.

Almost Perfect

Patriots **quarterback** Tom Brady faced history with a smile. Days before the 2008 **Super Bowl**, New York Giants receiver Plaxico Burress had said that not only would the Giants beat the undefeated New England Patriots, they'd also hold New England to just 17 points.

The Patriots had set a record by averaging 32 points a game. Tom had thrown for a record 50 **touchdown passes** and was the most valuable player in the **NFL** (National Football League). Patriots receiver Randy Moss had caught a record 23 touchdown passes.

"[I'd hope he'd give] us some credit for scoring some points," Tom said about Burress, with a grin.

The Patriots were trying to become the first NFL team to go 19-0. Tom was trying to join Terry Bradshaw and Joe Montana as the only quarterbacks to win four Super Bowls. All the Patriots had to do was beat New York, a team they had defeated 38-35 in the last game of the regular season.

Tom was all over the news before the Super Bowl. A female TV reporter from Mexico asked him to marry her. Tom said no. Photographers took pictures and a video of him wearing a walking boot on his right foot while limping to take flowers to his girlfriend at her New York apartment. He had a high ankle sprain. There were also reports he hurt his shoulder.

Jacksonville tried to stop him in the first playoff game by taking away the deep pass, so he threw short and set an NFL record by completing 26 of 28 passes (one pass was dropped) for 262 yards and three **touchdowns**. New England won. San Diego pressured him into three **interceptions** (in-ter-SEP-shuns)— and hurt his ankle while **sacking** him—but he

Tom Brady got a marriage proposal from Ines Gomez Mont of TV Azteca during New England's Super Bowl media day. Tom turned her down.

still threw two touchdown passes. New England won again to make it to the Super Bowl.

The Patriots were 12-point favorites over New York. But the Giants hit Tom like he hadn't been hit before. They sacked him five times, and knocked him down six more times. Still, Tom almost had another amazing finish after New York took a 10-7 lead late in the fourth quarter. He got New England close to the end zone, then looked to Moss, his favorite

Tom Brady just got off a pass before taking a big hit from New York defensive end Michael Strahan (#92) in Super Bowl XLII. The Giants hit Tom more than he'd been hit all season.

receiver. Moss beat defensive back Corey Webster for a 6-yard touchdown catch to give the Patriots a 14-10 lead with three minutes left and, it seemed, a perfect season.

Then the Giants spoiled it all. Quarterback Eli Manning hit Plaxico with a 13-yard touchdown pass with just 35 seconds left in the game. That wasn't enough time, even for Tom. The Giants won 17-14.

Still, many experts consider Tom the greatest quarterback ever. That's not bad for a guy who worries about his flaws. He has said, "I've never been the fastest or had the best arm or been very strong." And he once said he questioned whether "I'm really cut out for this. I think I am pretty insecure."

Insecure (in-seh-KYOOR) or not, in 2007 Tom had one of the greatest seasons in NFL history. That would have to be enough. For now.

Tom Brady warms up before leading Michigan against Arkansas in the 1999 Florida Citrus Bowl in Orlando, Florida. Michigan won 45-31.

Early Years

Thomas Edward Brady Jr. was born on August 3, 1977, in San Mateo, California. His parents, Tom Sr. and Galynn, already had three daughters—Maureen, Julie, and Nancy. Tom Sr. was a banker. Galynn was a stay-at-home mom. It was a sports-minded family. They were huge San Francisco 49ers and Giants fans, and played sports such as basketball. They were so **competitive** (kum-PEH-tih-tiv) that even today, they have hot salsa–eating contests to see who can eat the most salsa before taking a drink.

As a young boy, Tom was very competitive during games of football, baseball, capture the flag, and hide and seek. Sometimes he was too competitive, and he'd get angry when he lost. One time, he threw a video controller at a TV. Other times, he'd smash a tennis racket or break a golf club. Eventually, he learned to control his temper. That's when he became very good.

His football heroes were San Francisco 49ers quarterbacks Joe Montana and Steve Young. His baseball heroes were Wade Boggs, Don Mattingly, and Will Clark. He threw right-handed but tried to bat left-handed because Boggs, Mattingly, and Clark hit left-handed.

Tom starred at Junipero Serra High School. He was the starting catcher for the baseball team. He was good enough for Major League Baseball's Montreal Expos to pick him in the 18th round of the 1995 draft.

Tom didn't want to play pro baseball. He loved football. In high school he threw for 3,702 yards and 31 touchdowns and made the Prep Football Report All-America team. More than 75 schools recruited him. In the end, he chose Michigan. Yes, it was far from his California home, but it was a good school and a national power with great football **tradition** (truh-DIH-shun). It also had a stadium that held more than 110,000 people.

Tom Brady (#10) led Michigan to a 20-5 record his last two years. His last college pass went for a touchdown to beat Alabama in the 2000 Orange Bowl.

Not many Michigan fans knew Tom when he arrived. By the time he left, everybody knew him.

New England quarterbacks Drew Bledsoe (right) and Tom Brady run drills during a 2002 practice. Bledsoe was the starter until getting hurt in the second game. Brady took over, and the rest is history.

New England Winner

The New England coaches liked Tom because he was a winner and had a good attitude. They were surprised when he was still available in the sixth round with the number 199 pick. Coach Bill Belichick said Tom was a lot better than that—he should have been chosen much earlier.

New England had a good starting quarterback in Drew Bledsoe, but they needed a backup who might someday replace him. They drafted Tom for the job in the spring of 2000.

Tom didn't play that first season. He needed to lift weights to get bigger and stronger. He knew people doubted him, and he wanted to prove them wrong. Charlie Weis,

New England coach Bill Belichick congratulates Tom Brady after the Patriots won their 19th straight game in 2004. The streak included a Super Bowl victory.

who was then the Patriots **offensive coordinator** (koh-OR-dih-nay-tur) and who eventually became the Notre Dame coach, said Tom came into the league "with a bit of a chip on his shoulder. He thought he was better than NFL experts thought he was."

The next year Tom gained 30 pounds to weigh in at about 215. He started July training camp as the fourth-string quarterback. Soon he

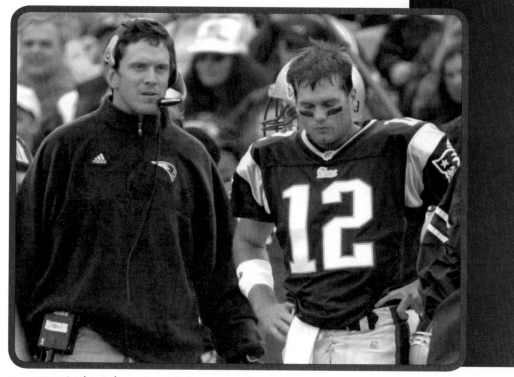

Tom Brady (right) replaced the injured Drew Bledsoe two games into the 2001 season and led the Patriots to a Super Bowl victory. Bledsoe never regained his starting job.

passed third-stringer Michael Bishop. Then he passed second-stringer Damon Huard, who had been signed to back up Bledsoe.

Bledsoe was hurt in the second game against the New York Jets and couldn't play for a couple of months. On September 23, 2001, Tom took over a 0-2 team. Some critics thought chances for a successful season were over. They were wrong.

17

Tom Brady holds one of his two Super Bowl Most Valuable Player trophies. He has led New England to four Super Bowls and three Super Bowl victories.

Super Bowl MVP

Tom doesn't have the strongest arm, but he is very **accurate** (AK-yur-it). In 2001 he set an NFL record by throwing his first 162 passes without an interception. He knows his limits. He is calm—his nickname is California Cool—and smart. He takes what defenses give him rather than forcing a pass that could lead to an interception. If the **defense** covers his receivers going deep, he throws short; if they cover his receivers going short, he throws deep.

To play quarterback, you have to be tough. You get hit hard by very large, very fast defensive players.

"Sometimes, getting up in the morning and brushing your teeth is the hardest part of the day," Tom said. "It all hurts."

Tom is shy off the field, but on the field, teammates say he is so **confident** (KON-fih-dent), he makes them believe they will win.

New England did win in the 2001 season. The team made the playoffs, beat Oakland in a snowstorm, then beat favored Pittsburgh for the AFC championship. Tom hurt his ankle in the second quarter of the game against Pittsburgh. He had completed 12 of 18 passes

Tom Brady overcame the snow and the Oakland Raiders defense to lead the Patriots to a comeback playoff victory in 2001. The "Snow Bowl" was the last game played at Foxboro Stadium.

for 115 yards. Bledsoe replaced him and led the Patriots to the victory. Bledsoe thought he should start in the Super Bowl against favored St. Louis, but Coach Belichick said no. Tom was healthy again. He would start.

Before the game, players were nervous. Some paced. Some prayed. Some threw up. Tom took a nap.

The score was tied 17-17 when the Patriots started on their own 17-yard line with 1 minute 21 seconds left and no timeouts. Tom completed pass after pass to get them close enough for Adam Vinatieri to kick the game-winning **field goal** as time expired. New England won 20-17, and Tom was named Super Bowl MVP.

Tom went to Disney World in Orlando, Florida, where he rode in a parade with Mickey Mouse. He also hung out with NFL Hall of Fame quarterback Dan Marino, Hall of Fame baseball player Willie Mays, and home run king Barry Bonds. He got so many calls he had to change his phone number three times.

Tom Brady's reward for winning Super Bowl XXXVI's Most Valuable Player award—New England upset favored St. Louis—was a trip to Disney World and a parade ride with Mickey Mouse at MGM Studios.

Tom and New England won the Super Bowl again in 2004. The Patriots beat Carolina 32-29 when Tom led another last-minute drive for the winning field goal. He was named MVP again. The Patriots also won the Super Bowl in 2005, beating Philadelphia 24-21. Tom threw for 236 yards and two touchdowns. Adam Vinatieri added the winning 22-yard field goal. No other quarterback had ever won three Super Bowls before his twenty-eighth birthday.

Tom is the ultimate winner. He set an NFL record by winning his first 10 playoff games. His playoff record is 14-3. He is 100-25 as a starter. He reached 100 wins faster than any other NFL quarterback in history.

Tom's previous success came without superstar receivers. That changed in 2007 when receivers such as Randy Moss and Donté Stallworth joined New England. Tom threw for more touchdowns and the Patriots scored more points than any quarterback or team had before. That season, they won everything but the Super Bowl.

Tom Brady visits with kids from the Make-A-Wish Foundation. He is involved in numerous charities, both nationally and in the New England area.

Role Model

Tom's success has made him wealthy. In 2005 he signed a six-year contract with the Patriots worth $60 million. He also does commercials for companies such as Nike, Sirius, and Visa. In 2006 he made $29 million, and *Forbes* magazine ranked him 52nd in earnings among the top 100 celebrities.

Tom hosted the TV show *Saturday Night Live* in 2005. *Esquire* magazine named him the Best Dressed Man in the World in 2007.

The gossip pages keep close tabs on his private life. In the summer of 2007, his girlfriend was supermodel Gisele Bundchen. His former girlfriend, actress Bridget Moynahan, gave birth to his son, John Edward Thomas Moynahan, on August 29 that year.

Tom says he understands his life is public, but he wishes the **tabloids** would leave his parents and sisters alone.

Tom is always trying to be a great role model. He's involved in several charities. In 2003 he worked with the Starlight Children's Foundation of New England, which helps seriously ill children. In 2004 he visited Walter Reed Medical Center in Washington, D.C., to cheer up soldiers injured in the Iraq war. He had an **audience** (AW-dee-ents) with Pope John Paul II in 2004. In 2005, *Sports Illustrated* named him its Sportsman of the Year. He made an eight-day trip to Africa in the spring of 2007. There, he visited health clinics and schools to promote the importance of good health and education.

Patriots owner Robert Kraft told *USA Today*, "There isn't a finer player in the NFL than Tom Brady, not only as a player, but as a human being."

Tom has a lot of talent, but more than that, he works hard, prepares hard, and always does his best.

Galynn and Tom Brady Senior accompany their son as he accepts his 2005 Sports Illustrated Sportsman of the Year award.

"A lot of times I find that people who are blessed with the most talent don't ever develop that competitive attitude," he said, "and the ones who aren't blessed in that way are the most competitive and have the bigger hearts."

Tom is talented *and* he has a big heart. That's why he is such a big winner.

CAREER STATS

Year	Team	G	GS	Comp	Att	Pct	Yards	YPA	Lg	TD	Int	Rate
2000	NE	1	0	1	3	33.3	6	2	6	0	0	42.4
2001	NE	15	14	264	413	63.9	2843	6.9	91	18	12	86.5
2002	NE	16	16	373	601	62.1	3764	6.3	49	28	14	85.7
2003	NE	16	16	317	527	60.2	3620	6.9	82	23	12	85.9
2004	NE	16	16	288	474	60.8	3692	7.8	50	28	14	92.6
2005	NE	16	16	334	530	63.0	4110	7.8	71	26	14	92.3
2006	NE	16	16	319	516	61.8	3529	6.8	62	24	12	87.9
2007	NE	16	16	398	578	68.9	4806	8.3	69	50	8	117.2
Total		112	110	2294	3642	63.0	23370	7.2	91	197	86	92.9

(G=Games, GS=Games started, Comp=Completions, Att=Attempts, Pct=Percentage, YPA=Yards per attempt, Lg=Longest pass, TD=Touchdown, Int=Interceptions, Rate=Quarterback rating)

CHRONOLOGY

1977 Tom Brady is born on August 3 in San Mateo, California.

1994 Tom finishes his high school career with 3,702 passing yards and 31 touchdowns, earning high school All-America honors.

1995 Tom signs with Michigan after being recruited by 75 schools. He is drafted by Major League Baseball's Montreal Expos in the 18th round, but sticks with football.

1999 He leaves Michigan with a 20-5 record as a starter. His last college pass is a touchdown that beats Alabama 35-34 in the Orange Bowl.

2000 He is drafted in the sixth round by the New England Patriots.

2001 Tom becomes the New England starter in September. He leads the Patriots to a 2002 Super Bowl victory over St. Louis and is named MVP.

2002 Tom leads the NFL with 28 touchdown passes.

2003 He leads New England to a 17-2 record and wins the 2004 Super Bowl (beating Carolina 32-29) and receives MVP honors again.

2005 New England beats Philadelphia 24-21 to win its third Super Bowl title in four years. Brady signs a six-year, $60 million contract. *Sports Illustrated* names Tom Sportsman of the Year.

2006 Tom runs his total to 24 game-winning drives in the fourth quarter or overtime. Six of those drives are in playoff games.

2007 His son, John Edward Thomas Moynahan, is born on August 29 to Bridget Moynahan. Tom wins MVP Award while setting record for most touchdown passes in a season (50).

2008 Tom leads New England past Jacksonville and San Diego to reach the Super Bowl for the fourth time in seven years. The New York Giants win, 17-14.

FIND OUT MORE

Books

Gigliotti, Jim. *Tom Brady* (World's Greatest Athletes). Elgin, Illinois: Child's World, 2007.

Savage, Jeff. *Tom Brady* (Amazing Athletes). Minneapolis: Lerner Publishing Co., 2006.

Stewart, Mark. *Tom Brady: Heart of the Huddle.* Brookfield, Connecticut, Millbrook Press, 2003.

Wheeler, Jill C. *Tom Brady* (Awesome Athletes). Edina, Minnesota: Checkerboard Books, 2006.

Works Consulted

Author's interview with John Borton, editor, *The Wolverine*, P.O. Box 1304 Ann Arbor, MI 48106; October 13, 2007.

"The Best Dressed Men in the World, 2007: Tom Brady." *Esquire*, August 23, 2007. http://www.esquire.com/style/fashion-story/bestdressed0907-2

Goldman, Lea, Monte Burke, and Kiri Blakeley (editors). "The Celebrity 100." *Forbes*, June 14, 2007, http://www.forbes.com/lists/2006/53/X66I.html

FIND OUT MORE

Holley, Michael. *Patriot Reign: Bill Belichick, the Coaches, and the Players Who Built a Champion*. New York: Harper Paperbacks, 2005.

McConaughey, Matthew. "Tom Brady: Were He Not the Star Quarterback of Football's Best Team, Tom Brady Might Have Been Coming Soon to a Theater Near You." *Interview*, October 2004, http://findarticles.com/p/articles/mi_m1285/is_9_34/ai_n6213158

Michigan Media Guide 2007. Ann Arbor: Spectrum Printers/University of Michigan Athletics Department, 2007.

New England Patriots On-Line Media Guide 2007. http://www.patriots.com/team/index.cfm?ac=playerbio&bio=566

Pedulla, Tom. "For Tom Brady, Changes Come On and Off the Field." *USA Today*, July 25, 2007, http://www.usatoday.com/sports/football/nfl/patriots/2007-06-05-brady-cover_N.htm

Weis, Charlie, and Vic Carucci. *No Excuses: One Man's Incredible Rise Through the NFL to Head Coach of Notre Dame*. New York: Harper Entertainment, 2007.

On the Internet

Tom Brady News
www.absolutebrady.com

Tom Brady: NFL Profile
http://www.nfl.com/players/tombrady/profile?id=BRA371156

Tom Brady: Official New England Patriots Player Page
http://www.patriots.com/team/index.cfm?ac=playerbio&bio=566

GLOSSARY

accurate (AK-yur-it)—Of a quarterback, able to throw the ball exactly where he wants it to go.

audience (AW-dee-ents)—A personal meeting, as with the Pope (the world leader of the Catholic Church).

competitive (kum-PEH-tih-tiv)—Having a strong desire and drive to win.

confident (KON-fih-dent)—Having trust in your own abilities.

defense (DEE-fents)—The team that is trying to keep the other team from scoring.

field goal (FEELD gohl)—A play in which the ball is kicked through the goalposts into the end zone; it is worth three points.

insecure (in-seh-KYOOR)—Not sure of yourself, lacking confidence.

interception (in-ter-SEP-shun)—A play in which a defensive player from the opposing team catches a quarterback's pass.

NFL—National Football League. The NFL is divided into two conferences, the American Football Conference (AFC) and the National Football Conference (NFC). The two best teams in each conference play for conference championships. The winners of these advance to the Super Bowl.

offensive coordinator (off-EN-siv koh-OR-dih-nay-tur)—The coach who runs the offense (scoring strategy) and calls the plays.

quarterback (KWAR-ter-bak)—The player who runs the offense and throws the passes.

sacking (SAK-ing)—Knocking down the quarterback before he throws the ball.

Super Bowl—The NFL championship game between the American Football Conference and the National Football Conference winners. It is held on a Sunday in late January or early February.

tabloids (TAA-bloyds)—Newspapers that report on celebrity gossip.

touchdown (TUTCH-down)—Moving the ball into the end zone; it is worth six points.

touchdown pass (TUTCH-down pass)—A pass that is caught in the end zone; it is worth six points.

tradition (truh-DIH-shun)—Something that has been repeated many times over a long history.

INDEX